Barnes (Florence) v. Commissioner of Internal Revenue U.S. Supreme Court Transcript of Record with Supporting Pleadings

GEORGE D CROWLEY, ERWIN N GRISWOLD

Barnes (Florence) v. Commissioner of Internal Revenue
Petition / GEORGE D CROWLEY / 1969 / 314 / 396 U.S. 836 / 90 S.Ct. 94 / 24 L.Ed.2d 86 / 7-5-1969
Barnes (Florence) v. Commissioner of Internal Revenue
Brief in Opposition (P) / ERWIN N GRISWOLD / 1969 / 314 / 396 U.S. 836 / 90 S.Ct. 94 / 24 L.Ed.2d 86 / 8-6-1969

Barnes (Florence) v. Commissioner of Internal Revenue U.S. Supreme Court Transcript of Record with Supporting Pleadings

Table of Contents

162

No. 314

In the
Supreme Court of the United States

OCTOBER TERM, 1969

FLORENCE M. BARNES, and BARNES THEATRE TICKET SERVICE, INC., an Illinois corporation,

Petitioners,

vs.

THE COMMISSIONER OF INTERNAL REVENUE,

Respondent.

PETITION FOR A WRIT OF CERTIORARI TO THE UNITED STATES COURT OF APPEALS FOR THE SEVENTH CIRCUIT

GEORGE D. CROWLEY
135 South LaSalle Street
Chicago, Illinois 60603
Attorney for Petitioners

CROWLEY, GOSCHI AND GRIFFIN
135 South LaSalle Street
Chicago, Illinois 60603
Of Counsel

UNITED STATES LAW PRINTING CO., CHICAGO, ILLINOIS 60618 (312) 525-6581

INDEX

CITATION OF AUTHORITIES

Cases

Rules of Court

In the
Supreme Court of the United States

OCTOBER TERM, 1969

No.

FLORENCE M. BARNES, and BARNES THEATRE TICKET
SERVICE, INC., an Illinois corporation,

Petitioners,

vs.

THE COMMISSIONER OF INTERNAL REVENUE,

Respondent.

PETITION FOR A WRIT OF CERTIORARI TO THE UNITED STATES COURT OF APPEALS FOR THE SEVENTH CIRCUIT

Florence M. Barnes and Barnes Theatre Ticket Service, Inc., an Illinois corporation, petitioners herein, pray that a writ of certiorari be issued to review the decision of the United States Court of Appeals for the Seventh Circuit in this case.

OPINIONS OF THE COURTS BELOW

The Memorandum Findings of Fact and Opinion of the Tax Court of the United States and Decision entered pursuant thereto reported at 26 TCM 1290, are reproduced as Appendix I to this Petition. The decision of the United States Court of Appeals for the Seventh Circuit reported at 408 F2d 65 is reproduced as Appendix II to this Petition and the order of said court denying a rehearing en banc is set forth as Appendix III.

JURISDICTION

The decision of the United States Court of Appeals was rendered March 5, 1969. The Petition For A Rehearing En Banc was denied April 10, 1969. The United States Court of Appeals issued its Mandate to the Tax Court of the United States on April 23, 1969. Pursuant to motion of Petitioners for a Stay of Mandate, treated by the Court of Appeals as a Motion For Recall and Stay of Mandate, said Mandate was recalled and stayed for a period of 30 days on May 12, 1969. The order entered pursuant to this motion is attached hereto as Appendix IV. Petitioners filed a subsequent Motion For Stay of Mandate and the Court of Appeals ordered said Mandate stayed until July 9, 1969. This order is attached hereto as Appendix V.

The jurisdiction of the Supreme Court of the United States is invoked under Title 28 United States Code, Section 1254.

QUESTIONS PRESENTED

1. Where the Commissioner of Internal Revenue determines that a portion of taxpayer's cost of goods sold are to be disallowed, does due process require disclosure by the Commissioner as to which transactions are challenged?

2. Whether the decision of the United States Court of Appeals for the Seventh Circuit is in conflict with the decision rendered by this Court in *Helvering* v. *Taylor*, 293 US 507 (1935)?

CONSTITUTIONAL AND STATUTORY PROVISIONS INVOLVED

The Due Process clause of the Fifth Amendment to the Constitution of the United States, Title 26 United States Code Section 6212(a) Title 26 United States Code, Section 7453; Tax Court Rules of Practice Rule 32, reproduced as Appendix VI hereto.

STATEMENT OF THE CASE

On December 27, 1963 the Petitioners received a notice of deficiency (Appendix VII) which set forth a total deficiency in income taxes of $88,663.60 for the years 1955 through 1958. This deficiency was allegedly due to an overstatement of costs of operations as follows:

Year	Claimed	Allowed	Overstatement Cost of Operations
1955	$569,785.75	$499,010.61	$70,775.14
1956	499,164.30	436,451.28	62,713.02
1957	391,912.95	370,077.06	21,835.89
1958	475,372.89	460,929.65	14,443.24

The notice of deficiency did not specify which cost figures were challenged. The Petitioners sought to contest this determination in the Tax Court and to this end introduced their entire bookkeeping system into evidence as well as the testimony of their bookkeeper. The Commissioner did not at or during trial give further particulars as to disallowed costs. The Commissioner did not introduce at or during trial evidence in support of his determinations.

The United States Court of Appeals for the Seventh Circuit affirmed, J. Swygert dissenting, and denied a Petition for Rehearing En Banc.

Jurisdiction of the Tax Court is based on Title 26 United States Code Sections 7442 and 6213 (a) reproduced as Appendix VIII hereto.

REASONS RELIED ON FOR ALLOWANCE
OF THE WRIT

I.

THE PETITIONERS WERE DEPRIVED OF DUE PROCESS OF LAW IN VIOLATION OF THE FIFTH AMENDMENT TO THE CONSTITUTION OF THE UNITED STATES.

A.

The Application Of The Presumption Of Correctness To The Notice Of Deficiency Deprived The Petitioners Of Procedural Due Process Of Law.

The Court of Appeals in this case held that a notice of deficiency need only advise a taxpayer that the Commissioner means to assess him. Once this is done, a presumption of correctness is raised in favor of this determination and the burden of proof is placed on the taxpayer. (App. 27). The Commissioner need only disclose the amount of the deficiency—he is not required to disclose its basis, method of computation or even what items specifically are being challenged.

This decision has declared open season on all taxpayers. As J. Swygert indicated in his dissent, (App. 35), there is nothing to prevent the Commissioner from pulling a figure out of the reaches of his imagination and proceeding to enforce it if the taxpayer's books are not sufficient to disprove every possible theory of taxation. (App. 31). The Petitioners submit that they have a right to know wherein they have allegedly failed. The failure of the notice of deficiency so to inform the taxpayers in this case required them to grope in the fog through a Tax Court

trial in the hope that they might grasp something identifiable. To hold that the notice of deficiency in such a
case is presumed correct and that the taxpayer has the
burden of proof can only result in a deprivation of due
process in violation of the Fifth Amendment to the Constitution of the United States.

Although due process is not capable of reduction to a
simple formula or precise definition, it is susceptible to
empirical definition within the framework of decisional law.
''Fairness'' and ''fair play'' may be said to be the touch-
stone of procedural due process; *Joint Anti-Fascist Ref-
ugee Comm.* v. *McGrath*, 341 U.S. 123, 161, (1950); *Kin-
sella* v. *United States*, 361 U.S. 234, (1960). Protection
of the individual from arbitrary action is the essence of
due process, *Slochower* v. *Board of Higher Education of
New York City*, 350 U.S. 551 (1955).

Individuals are entitled to a fair hearing on the fundamental facts before their property is taken under the
edict of an administrative officer, *McGrath, supra*, p. 162.

In *Green* v. *McElroy*, 360 U.S. 474, (1959) this Court
stated:

> ''It is an immutable principle of jurisprudence that
> where governmental action seriously injures an in-
> dividual and the reasonableness of the action depends
> on fact findings, the evidence used to prove the gov-
> ernment's case, documentary evidence and even more
> important testimony, must be disclosed to the individ-
> ual so that he has an opportunity to show that it is
> untrue.''

The well entrenched principles of due process as an-
nounced by this Court in decision after decision have been
abandoned in the consideration of this case by the courts

below. They have instead clung to narrow procedural rules the application of which have denied the Petitioners herein of a fair hearing upon the fundamental facts.

B.

The Requirement That The Taxpayers Show That The Deficiencies Were Computed In An Improper Manner Or That Their Books And Records Accurately Reflected Their Income Deprived The Petitioners Of Procedural Due Process Of Law.

The Court of Appeals stated in its opinion that "The critical question arises, as stated by the Tax Court, whether taxpayers adduced sufficient evidence showing that the asserted deficiencies were computed in an improper manner or by showing that its books and records adequately and accurately reflected its income, or by producing a combination of such evidence." (App. 28).

The Petitioners could not show that the deficiencies were computed in an improper manner because disallowed cost items giving rise to the deficiencies were never disclosed and hence the manner was not known. The effect of the Court's position was to place upon the Petitioners the burden of introducing books and records which in their entirety could conclusively disprove the asserted deficiency. By the Court's own measure, the Petitioners were deprived of one of two elemental methods of proof, that is, the introduction of evidence showing that the deficiencies were improperly computed. The Petitioners contend that the application of this "critical question" to this case deprived Petitioners of due process of law under the Fifth Amendment to the Constitution of the United States.

II.

THE DECISION OF THE UNITED STATES COURT OF APPEALS FOR THE SEVENTH CIRCUIT IS CONTRARY TO THE DECISION OF THIS COURT IN HELVERING v. TAYLOR, 293 U.S. 507 (1935).

In *Barnes,* out of hundreds of substantially identical ticket purchases totaling almost two million dollars over a four-year period, the Commissioner has determined that a portion of each year's total purchases should be disallowed. The notice of deficiency issued by the Commissioner which set forth these disallowances failed to disclose the challenged transactions. The Commissioner failed to offer evidence in support of his position at trial. The Petitioners introduced their entire set of books at trial in an attempt to substantiate their cost of goods sold figures. The Court of Appeals affirmed the holding of the Tax Court that the notice of deficiency was sufficient to raise the presumption of correctness and to place the burden of proof on the taxpayers. Petitioners contend that the notice of deficiency in this case was arbitrary and without apparent rational foundation under the rule of *Helvering* v. *Taylor,* 293 U.S. 507 (1935). The holding of the United States Court of Appeals for the Seventh Circuit in this matter is contrary to the holding of that case.

In *Helvering,* the taxpayer purchased all the stock of four utilities at a total cost of $96,030. He then organized a holding company to which the utilities' stock was transferred in exchange for all the shares of the holding company, to wit: 1,000 shares of no par value preferred entitled to $100 on liquidation; 2500 shares of no par value class A common; 5000 shares of no par value class B common having the voting power.

The holding company subsequently sold the utilities' stock to another corporation for $194,930.16. Later in the year, the holding company retired all of taxpayer's preferred stock paying him $99,000 therefore. In his 1928 return, the taxpayer ascribed the entire price paid for the utilities' company stock ($96,030) as the basis for the preferred holding company stock, and reported the difference of $2,970 as his gain on the sale.

The Commissioner took the position that the taxpayer was not entitled to charge the cost of all the stock to preferred and apportioned to preferred a cost based on the ratio of the amount the taxpayer received on retirement of preferred to the total received on the sale by the holding company multiplied by the taxpayer's original cost. Thus of the $96,030 paid for the utilities' stock, $48,771.16 was chargeable to the preferred. A gain of $50,228.84 was imputed to the taxpayer upon which the Commissioner determined a deficiency of $9,156.69.

The Board of Tax Appeals, without specific findings of fact made the same determination. The taxpayer failed to prove facts from which a correct determination could be made. The Court of Appeals held the determination excessive and since the evidence did not show the correct amount remanded the case for further proceedings.

The question presented on petition for Writ of Certiorari was:

"Whether the Circuit Court of Appeals erred in remanding this case to the Board of Tax Appeals for a new hearing on the ground that the Commissioner's determination of the amount of income was incorrect, although the taxpayer had failed to prove facts from which a correct determination could be made."

Thus, as stated at p. 511 of the opinion, the appellate court rightly held the evidence sufficient to require a finding that the Commissioner's apportionment, and hence determination, were unfair and erroneous, even though the taxpayer failed to establish the correct amount.

The Supreme Court rejected the Commissioner's contention that since the taxpayer failed to establish facts on which a fair apportionment could be made, the Commissioner's determinations should be sustained. The Court held at p. 514:

> "We find nothing in the statutes, the rules of the board or our decisions that gives any support to the idea that the commissioner's determination shown to be without rational foundation and excessive will be enforced unless the taxpayer proves he owes nothing or, if liable at all, shows the correct amount. While decisions of the lower courts may not be harmonious, our attention has not been called to any that persuasively supports the rule for which the commissioner here contends.

> "Unquestionably the burden of proof is on the taxpayer to show that the commissioner's determination is invalid. (citations omitted). Frequently, if not quite generally, evidence adequate to overthrow the commissioner's finding is also sufficient to show the correct amount, if any, that is due (citations omitted). But, where as in this case the taxpayer's evidence show the commissioner's determination to be arbitrary and excessive it may not reasonably be held that he is bound to pay a tax that confessedly he does not owe, unless his evidence was sufficient also to establish the correct amount that lawfully might be charged against him. On the facts shown by the taxpayer in this case, the board should have held the apportionment arbitrary and the commissioner's determination invalid.

> "Then, upon appropriate application that further hearing be had, it should have heard evidence to show whether a fair apportionment might be made and, if so, the correct amount of the tax."

The Petitioners herein similarly contend that the Commissioner's determinations are arbitrary on their face, without rational foundation and therefore could not be presumed correct. This contention is based on the failure of the Commissioner to disclose which purchases of tickets were disallowed. The Court of Appeals largely ignored this position and simply held: "We find no prejudice to taxpayers resulting from the form of the statutory notices." (App. 27).

The Petitioners contend that this holding is directly contrary to that of *Helvering* v. *Taylor, supra*, when this Court held that the Commissioner's determination is arbitrary when examined by itself and for what it is rather than to determine arbitrariness by an examination of the Petitioners' books to ascertain whether they give a foundation for a correct determination.

The Petitioners contend that the Commissioner's determinations were arbitrary. The question of the sufficiency of the taxpayers' books and records should not have been reached.

III.

THE QUESTIONS AND ISSUES PRESENTED ARE OF FUNDAMENTAL IMPORTANCE AND STAND IN GREAT NEED OF CLARIFICATION.

The broad question of what renders a Commissioners determination arbitrary has not been addressed by the Supreme Court since 1935, the date of the *Helvering* decision. The precise question of the degree of disclosure required in a Notice of Deficiency has never come before the Supreme Court and is in desperate need of clarification. Standards must be established in this area that are both consistent with due process and this Court's decision in *Helvering, supra*.

The various Circuit Courts of Appeal and courts of original jurisdiction, while generating much dicta, have contributed nothing significantly helpful. Cases in support of the proposition that no special form for a statutory notice of deficiency is required have been cited by the Commissioner. While some of these cases do contain language to that effect, an examination of the issues decided and the factual situations involved will disclose material factors which provide ample ground for distinguishing those cases from the one at hand.

Thus, in *Commissioner* v. *Forest Glen Creamery Co.* (CA7 1938) 98 F2d 968, the issue was whether a deficiency notice for a year not set forth on the face of the notice but in an addendum thereto constituted a proper notice for that year. The Court held that no particular form was required for the notice and that information contained in the addendum was sufficient to apprise the taxpayer of the year in question. A similar holding is contained in *McDonnell* v. *United States* (Ct. Cl. 1932) 59 F2d 290 where the issue was whether the Commissioner was required to advise the taxpayer in the deficiency notice that he had a right to institute proceedings before the Board of Tax Appeals.

The Commissioner also cites cases in support of his contention that the failure to explain how a given deficiency was determined has no effect on the validity of the statutory notice. In each of those cases[1] full disclosure was made to the taxpayer either at or before trial.

---

[1] *Commissioner* v. *Stewart* (CA 6 1951) 186 F2d 239.
Standard Oil Co. v. *Commissioner* (1941) 43 BTA 1941.
Finder v. *Commissioner* (1961) 37 TC 411.
Troiano v. *Commissioner* (1964) 23 TCM 1418.

Nowhere are there found factors such as are present in this case, namely the unexplained disallowance of a portion of taxpayer's cost of goods sold coupled with the failure of the Commissioner to disclose before or at trial exactly what had been disallowed or to produce any evidence at trial relative to his determination.

The decision of the Court of Appeals in this case has turned the burden of proof rule, meant to be a shield for the Tax Court[2] into a powerful sword in the hands of the Commissioner. As a result of this decision the Commissioner's determinations have been placed in an almost impregnable fortress, unassailable by a mere preponderance of evidence in favor of the taxpayer. The opportunity to show the Commissioner's determination arbitrary has practically disappeared and the taxpayer must now sustain the validity of his position beyond all reasonable doubt.

The present state of the law in this area can only be clarified under the guiding hand of the Supreme Court so "that traditional forms of fair procedure not be restricted by implication or without the most explicit action by the Nation's lawmakers, even in areas where it is possible that the Constitution presents no inhibition." *Green* v. *McElroy*, 360 US 474, 508.

---

[2] "The burden of proof rule is a necessary rule if the Tax Court is to dispose of the large number of cases which are inadequately presented: the Tax Court cannot be expected in view of its arduous duties, affirmatively to seek out evidence and prove taxpayer's cases for them." Mertens, *Law Of Federal Income Taxation*, Volume 9 Sections 50, 60.

In granting the application this tribunal puts the Commissioner in the enviable position of being fair with taxpayers without costing the government any money.

If there is validity in their disallowances as clearly delineated in notices, the Commissioner will prevail.

If there is no validity in disallowances the basis of which is not identifiable he should not exact the tax dollar unfairly.

Conclusion

For the reasons stated herein, the Petitioners earnestly pray that a writ of certiorari issue from this Court to review the judgment of the United States Court of Appeals for the Seventh Circuit in this case.

Respectfully submitted,

GEORGE D. CROWLEY
Chicago, Illinois
Attorney for Petitioners

CROWLEY, GOSCHI & GRIFFIN
Of Counsel

APPENDIX

APPENDIX I

Opinion Of The Tax Court

MEMORANDUM FINDINGS OF FACTS AND OPINION

IN THE TAX COURT OF THE UNITED STATES
* * (Caption—Nos. 1212-64 and 1210-64) * *

1. *Held*: Petitioner has failed to prove that its costs of operations for the years 1955 through 1958 exceeded the amounts allowed by the Commissioner.

2. *Held*: Petitioner has proved that it did not receive income on sales made to other ticket brokers during such years.

3. *Held*: A withdrawal of funds by Florence M. Barnes from the corporation in 1958 constituted the repayment of funds previously loaned by her to it.

George D. Crowley and *Gerald C. Risner*, for the petitioners.

Helen Viney Porter and *George T. Donoghue, Jr.*, for the respondent.

Simpson, *Judge*: The respondent determined deficiencies in income tax of the petitioners and additions to the tax as follows:

Cases of the following petitioners are consolidated herewith: Albert C. Eckhardt and Cassandra Eckhardt, docket No. 1211-64; and Florence M. Barnes, docket No. 1212-64.

Petitioner	Year	Deficiency	Additions to the tax[2]
Barnes Theatre Ticket Service, Inc.	1955	$32,763.18	—
,,	1956	33,295.98	—
,,	1957	11,175.89	—
,,	1958	11,428.55	—
Florence M. Barnes	1953	7,162.01	$ 358.10
,,	1955	14,503.54	725.18
,,	1956	44,584.03	2,655.00
,,	1957	15,561.75	778.09
,,	1958	36,892.42	1,844.62
Albert C. Eckardt and Cassandra Eckardt	1955	38,377.84	1,918.89
,,	1956	28,769.98	1,440.17
,,	1957	8,698.23	434.91
,,	1958	5,978.14	298.91

The respondent's adjustment of income tax of Florence M. Barnes for the year 1953 was the result of the elimination of a net operating loss reflected on her return for 1955. Part of the adjustments in income tax of Barnes Theatre Ticket Service, Inc., for the years 1955 and 1958 was the result of the elimination of net operating losses reflected on its returns for the years 1955 and 1956. The validity of these adjustments depends upon our decision as to other issues in the case, and such adjustments shall be taken care of in the Rule 50 computations.

There are basically three issues for decision. First, whether Barnes Theater Ticket Service, Inc., overstated its costs of operations for the taxable years 1955, 1956,

[2] Under section 293(a) of the Internal Revenue Code of 1939 and section 6653(a) of the Internal Revenue Code of 1954.

1957, and 1958.[2] Second, whether Barnes Theatre Ticket Service, Inc., realized gross income from sales to other ticket brokers in the taxable years 1955 through 1958. Third, whether a payment by Barnes Theatre Ticket Service, Inc., to Florence M. Barnes in 1958 is taxable to her as a dividend or whether such payment was in repayment of a loan previously made by her.

FINDINGS OF FACT

Some of the facts were stipulated, and those facts are so found.

Barnes Theatre Ticket Service, Inc. (Barnes), is a corporation with its principal place of business during the years 1955 through 1958, and at the time its petition was filed in this case, at Chicago, Illinois. Florence M. Barnes (Florence) is an individual who resided in Chicago, Illinois, during the years 1953 and 1955 through 1958 and at the time her petition was filed in this case. Albert C. Eckhardt (Albert) and Cassandra Eckhardt are individuals who resided in Northbrook, Illinois, during the years 1955 through 1958. All of the petitioners filed their Federal income tax returns for the years at issue in this case with the district director of internal revenue, Chicago, Illinois.

Barnes was incorporated under the laws of the State of Illinois on January 1, 1947. Its paid-in capital at the date of incorporation was $15,000. Florence, since the date of incorporation, has been the sole stockholder of Barnes. The officers of Barnes for the years 1955 through 1958 were Florence, President; Albert, Treasurer; and David Basofin, Vice President.

---

[2] *The Commissioner asserted deficiencies against both Flo etc & Eck, in amounts equal to the alleged overstated purchases for said years, contending that these taxpayers realized additional income from Barnes Theatre etc.*

Barnes is engaged in the business of reselling tickets for profit. It delivers to its customers tickets or cards of admission to theatres, operas, movies, sporting events, and other places of amusement at a charge in excess of established box office prices. This business is commonly known as that of a ticket broker.

During the years 1955 through 1958, Barnes purchased tickets for resale from the box offices of various theatres and sporting areas and from persons or organizations engaged in the production of various theatrical and sporting events. Barnes also purchased tickets by mail and from other people not regularly engaged in the business of selling tickets.

During the years 1955 through 1958, Barnes' principal office was located at the Palmer House Hotel. It was from this office that the purchase and sale of all tickets was controlled, and it was here that Florence, Albert, and Anne Magner (Anne), the bookkeeper, were located. Tickets were sold from a counter adjacent to the corporate offices in the Palmer House and from stands in a number of hotels and private clubs in the Chicago area.

Each day, the main office of Barnes received from each of the stands a sheet showing the date, the number of tickets sold by the stand, the number of tickets returned, the amount of money received, the customer's name, the theatres to which the tickets applied, and an inventory of tickets. The sheets did not show any amounts described as the cost of the tickets to Barnes or the premium over established box office price, if any, that Barnes paid for the tickets. The proceeds of the day's sales accompanied the sheets from each stand. The proceeds were then checked with the sheets and entered in Barnes' Cash Receipts book. Check proceeds from sales were deposited in Barnes' bank account, and currency was either deposited in the bank or maintained in the office safe as an operating fund.

Box office personnel located in various theatres and sporting arenas selected choice seat locations for each attraction being shown and sent the tickets of admission for such seats to the Palmer House office of Barnes or requested that its messenger pick them up at the box office. When Barnes received tickets from the treasurers of the various box offices, included with the tickets was a slip of paper showing the cost per ticket, the number of tickets purchased, and the amount of premium, if any, over the box office price paid by Barnes. After recording some of this information in the books and records, Anne destroyed the slip of paper. Box office personnel allowed Barnes to return tickets for full refund to the time of the performance.

At the end of each month, the daily sheets received from Barnes' various stands were "recapped", or summarized, by Anne. She then made quarter recaps from the monthly recaps which were used as a basis for computing sales in the preparation of Barnes' Federal excise tax returns. The sales figures on the quarterly recaps did not represent total sales but only those sales on which an excise tax was due.

For the year 1955, cash purchases by Barnes per week per theatre or event were recorded in its Cash Receipts book. For the years 1956, 1957, and 1958, total cash purchases for periods varying from one to several weeks were recorded in the Cash Receipts book. Although most purchases were paid for by cash, some were paid for by check. The amounts of such checks were recorded for the years 1955 through 1958 in the Cash Disbursements book.

The numbers of tickets purchased and sold by Barnes can be computed only from the daily sheets that the various stands kept; no totals or recaps were maintained by Barnes showing the total number of tickets purchased or sold during a particular year. The books and records of Barnes do not include any original entries as to costs of individual tickets purchased and the names of persons from whom purchases were made.

On occasions when the current operating funds of Barnes were insufficient to pay for cash ticket purchases, Florence supplied funds to enable it to make such purchases. On Barnes' books, these funds advanced by Florence were treated as loans. The following schedule shows totals taken from its books regarding the funds advanced by Florence during the years 1954 through 1958 and the repayments to Florence:

Year	Advanced by Florence	Repaid to Florence
1954	$ 6,000.00	$ -0-
1955	31,200.00	640.66
1956	28,350.00	29,000.00
1957	12,000.00	7,800.00
1958	-0-	40,109.34
	$77,550.00	$77,550.00

Barnes' books do not, for the most part, reflect the dates funds were advanced or the amounts of funds advanced by Florence on such dates; rather, the book entries regarding such funds appear to be year-end summaries of various transactions that took place during the year.

During the years 1955 through 1957, Barnes received bundles of tickets from various box offices for transmittal to other ticket brokers. Each bundle of tickets was accompanied by a slip of paper indicating the ticket broker to whom such tickets were to be transmitted and the amount of money to be paid to each box office for such tickets. The ticket broker, upon his receipt of the tickets, paid Barnes for the tickets, and Barnes in turn paid the box office from which the tickets came.

There is no record in Barnes' books of the acquisition of any large capital assets or of the payment of any dividends to Florence or Albert in any of the years 1955 through 1958.

On its returns, Barnes reported gross receipts of $752,357.57 for the taxable year 1955, $675,900.60 for 1956, $592,502.50 for 1957, and $737,959.74 for 1958. Barnes reported total costs of operations of $569,785.75 for 1955, $499,164.30 for 1956, $391,912.95 for 1957, and $475,372.89 for 1958. The respondent disallowed as costs of operations $70,775.14 for 1955, $62,813.02 for 1956, $21,835.89 for 1957, and $14,443.24 for 1958.

Barnes' books and records show that it purchased tickets for transmittal to other ticket brokers in the amounts of $58,205.45 for the taxable year 1955, $83,877.30 for 1956, $19,056.70 for 1957, and $8,493.80 for 1958. The books and records further show that Barnes' sales to other ticket brokers for the taxable years 1955 through 1958 were in the same amounts as its purchases, resulting in no income to Barnes. The respondent in his determination reduced the amounts of Barnes' purchases for sale to other ticket brokers to $48,504.54 for the taxable year 1955, $69,897.75 for 1956, $15,880.59 for 1957, and $7,078.17 for 1958.

OPINION

The major issue in this case is the amount of Barnes' costs of operations for the years 1955 through 1958. In the first place, Barnes challenges the validity of the notice of deficiency. In the notice, the respondent set forth that he was disallowing a portion of the costs of operations for lack of substantiation, but the respondent did not indicate how he arrived at that portion. Barnes contends that such notice is insufficient to give rise to the presumption of correctness. However, we believe that the notice is sufficient to be entitled to the presumption of correctness. See, *Commissioner* v. *Stewart*, 186 F. 2d 239 (C.A. 6, 1951), revg. on other grounds a Memorandum Opinion of this Court; *Albert D. McGrath*, 27 T.C. 117 (1956). Cf., *Marx* v. *Commissioner*, 179 F. 2d 938 (C.A. 1, 1950), affg. a Memorandum Opinion of this Court, cert. denied 339 U.S. 964 (1950); *Estate of Peter Finder*, 37 T.C. (1961). In so holding, we are not approving of the deficiency; we are merely saying that the notice of deficiency is sufficient to raise the presumption of correctness and to place the burden of proof on the petitioners.

Barnes also raises an issue as to the effect of such presumption. The language sometimes used in discussing the presumption may be confusing, but clearly, the petitioner has the responsibility of persuading us that the asserted deficiency is erroneous or arbitrary. *Welch* v. *Helvering*, 290 U.S. 111 (1933); *Archer* v. *Commissioner*, 227 F. 2d 270 (C.A. 5, 1955), affg. a Memorandum Opinion of this Court; *Duquesne Steel Foundry Co.*, 15 B.T.A. 467 (1929), affd. per curiam 41 F. 2d 995 (C.A. 3, 1930), affd. per curiam 283 U.S. 799 (1931). The decisions which appear to contain inconsistent language as to the procedural aspects of this rule do not affect the validity of the rule. Compare *United Airline Company* v. *Commissioner*, 316 F. 2d 701 (C.A. 1, 1963), affg. a Memorandum Opinion of this Court, with *Stout* v. *Commissioner*, 273 F. 2d 345 (C.A. 4, 1959), revg. a Memorandum Opinion of this Court.

To prevail, Barnes need not establish the amount of its tax liability. *Helvering* v. *Taylor*, 293 U.S. 507 (1935). It can succeed by showing that the asserted deficiency was computed in an improper manner or by showing that its books and records are adequate and accurately reflect its income, or by producing a combination of such evidence. *H. T. Rainwater*, 23 T.C. 450 (1954); *Morris Nemmo*, 24 T.C. 583 (1955). Barnes has adduced no evidence as to the manner in which the respondent computed the asserted deficiency; instead, it rests its case on an attempt to show that its books are reliable and correctly reflect its income.

In its Cash Receipts book and its Cash Disbursements books, the entries for 1955 merely show the total amount spent for the purchase of tickets at a particular theatre or box office over a period of a week or more. For the later years involved in this case, the Cash Receipts book does not even show the theatre or box office at which the tickets were purchased. The invoices which accompanied the purchases have been destroyed. Except for the recaps for 1957, there are generally no entries showing the names of the persons from whom tickets were purchased, the dates of the purchases, and the amounts paid for particular tickets or groups of tickets. Although the recaps for 1957 include some of such information, it is not clear how they were prepared; they were apparently prepared from the daily reports from the stands, and not from the invoices accompanying the purchases. We find these books and records to be inadequate to establish Barnes' costs of operations. In view of the destruction of the invoices, there is no way of verifying the correctness of the totals. *Jack Showell*, 23 T.C. 495 (1954, remd. on other grounds 238 F. 2d 148 (C.A. 9, 1956).

Moreover, in this case, we do not have supporting testimony of the nature provided in the *Rainwater* and *Nemmo* cases, *supra*. In those cases, the testimony established a convincing chain of evidence. The Court was told how the original entries were prepared, how they were copied on to a summary, and how that summary was transferred to other books. In addition, the books and summaries were then used as a basis for a business decision: In the *Rainwater case*, a division of partnership profits was predicated on the books and summaries; in the *Nemmo* case, substantial amounts of operating cash were given to an employee on the basis of the books and summaries. Thus, if the Court found the testimony credible, it then followed that the summaries should be reliable. In the case before us, we are merely told that Anne copied the invoice information and then destroyed them. We are not told on what documents she copied the information; we are not told how she computed the totals which were included in the books; we are not told how she arrived at the figures which appear in the recaps; and we have not been shown that any business decisions were based upon the books and records. Under such circumstances, we have little to convince us that the totals are reliable.

Finally, a very dark cloud is cast on the reliability of the cost information in the books by statements which Florence made to the agent of the respondent during the investigation of the tax liabilities of Barnes. According to the agent, Florence told him that the records of Barnes did not reflect the true cost of the tickets. She stated that the figures for purchases in the books also included other costs and that she would give Ann the figures for costs of tickets to place in the books. She also stated that she made payments to State legislators to prevent the passage of unfavorable legislation, and that such payments were included on the books and records of Barnes in the figures for purchases.

Barnes counsel objected to the admission of this testimony claiming that it was inadmissible hearsay. According to his argument, the agent was engaged in an excise tax liability investigation, and since the admissions were made in connection with that investigation, they were not admissible in an income tax controversy. However, we have concluded that the testimony as to Florence's statements is admissible. It is not clear whether the investigation was confined to excise tax liability, and even if it was so limited, such fact does not prevent the admission of the statements in this income tax proceeding. Her statements are clearly relevant to this controversy, and the reasons for allowing the admission of such statements are all present. Florence cannot complain that her statements to the agent were not trustworthy, nor can she object to their admission because of a lack of opportunity for cross-examination. See, McCormick, Evidence, pp. 502-504 (1954).

Florence's statements constitute additional reasons for doubting the reliability of the cost information contained in the Barnes' records. See, *Albert D. McGrath, supra.* Florence, although she was at the trial, did not take the stand, and no effort was made to explain away the doubts raised by her statements to the agent.

Frankly, we realize that Barnes' failure to keep better records may have been innocent and that the consequence of our conclusion imposes a heavy tax burden on Barnes. Yet, the corporation was engaged in a large business, and inasmuch as the business involved largely cash transactions, it seems that Barnes should have recognized the necessity of keeping more complete records. In view of the failure to retain the records necessary to enable a verification of the ultimate totals, the failure to support the totals with a showing of the systematic compilation of information, and the doubts cast on the records by Florence's statements, we feel compelled to conclude that Barnes has failed to persuade us that its books and records accurately reflect its costs of operations.

The respondent also determined that Barnes had gross income from the sale of tickets to other ticket brokers for the years 1955 through 1958. It is Barnes' position that sales to other ticket brokers were "wash sales"; that it merely picked up the tickets at the various box offices, and the brokers paid Barnes whatever it had paid the box office. These transactions were reflected on Barnes' books as wash sales. On the other hand, the respondent contends that the figures representing the purchases on these purported wash sales cannot be substantiated and that the amount of purchases was less than the amount of sales, resulting in gross income to Barnes.

The information contained in Barnes' books and records regarding the purchases and sales to other brokers is significantly different. The original documents, that is the invoices, have also been destroyed. However, the books contain information relating to each transaction. Such information includes the name of the source from whom the tickets were purchased, the person to whom they were sold, the amount paid for the tickets, the amount received for them, and the date of the transaction. Moreover, Anne, whose testimony we found credible, testified that she entered this information in the books contemporaneously with the purchase and sale of the tickets for other brokers. In view of the more detailed information in the books and the testimony that these entries were made contemporaneously, we hold that the books are sufficient evidence to establish the costs and selling prices for these transactions and that Barnes realized no income from them.

The respondent further determined that Florence received income from Barnes in the amount of $40,109.34 as a result of Barnes transferring that amount to her in 1958. The respondent states that Florence's withdrawal of this amount from the corporate funds was actually a distribution of a dividend, but Florence contends that the transfer was a repayment of loans which she had made to the corporation.

The books and records of Barnes show that over the years Florence several times advanced funds to Barnes and several times withdrew funds. For the years 1954 through 1957, the books show that in each year the advances were almost equal to or greater than the withdrawals. But for 1958, the books show that Florence made no advances and withdrew $40,109.34. Overall, for the years 1954 through 1958, the books show that total advances equaled total withdrawals.

There is a question as to whether the information in Barnes' books and records in regard to the advances and withdrawals by Florence is reliable. In view of the testimony regarding the advances and withdrawals and the fact that the books record withdrawals as well as advances, we have concluded that the books are reliable and sufficient to establish that such advances and withdrawals did in fact occur.

The book entries of Barnes stated that the amounts that Florence advanced were "loans payable" to Florence. However, no notes were issued by Barnes to Florence, and no interest was ever due or paid. The respondent, therefore, argues that the book entries, are insufficient to establish that in fact the advances were loans and not capital contributions. The respondent further argues that Barnes was undercapitalized since it only had total capital ranging from about $22,000 to about $55,000 in the years 1955 through 1958 as compared to average annual purchases of over $400,000.

Whether an advance of funds and subsequent withdrawal by a stockholder of a corporation is a loan and repayment or a contribution to capital and dividend depends upon the intent of the parties at the time the advances and withdrawals were made. *2554-58 Creston Corp.*, 40 T.C. 932 (1963). Stated differently, the question is whether Florence advanced the funds to Barnes with reasonable expectations of repayment regardless of the success of the venture or whether she placed the funds at the risk of the business. *Gilbert* v. *Commissioner*, 248 F. 2d 399 (C.A. 2, 1957), remg. a Memorandum Opinion of this Court. We must infer the intent of the parties from a consideration of all of the facts and circumstances surrounding the transaction. *Leach Corporation*, 30 T.C. 563 (1958).

An important factor in determining whether funds were to be placed at the risk of Barnes' business is the adequacy of the equity capital of that business. There should be a sufficient capital cushion to absorb a reasonable portion of the risk of loss of the funds. Barnes did have throughout the years in question $22,000 or more in equity capital. The respondent contends that this amount was insufficient to conduct Barnes' business. While Barnes' annual purchases exceeded $400,000, its inventory turned over rapidly. Since unsold tickets could be returned to the box office, Barnes carried little or no permanent or continuing inventory. Such a rapid turnover of inventory makes the respondent's comparison of equity capital to cost of goods sold less meaningful.

We believe that we must also reject the respondent's argument that since no notes were issued by Barnes to Florence and no interest was ever due or paid, the amounts advanced to Barnes were not loans. The advances were carried on Barnes' books as "loans payable". In view of the fact that Florence was the sole stockholder of Barnes, the informality and lack of an interest provision is not surprising. See, *Irving T. Bush*, 45 B.T.A. 609 (1941), revd. on other grounds 133 F. 2d 1005 (C.A. 2, 1943).

The decisive consideration, in our view, is that repayment could have been expected within a relatively short time and did in fact occur within such time. Because of the rapid turnover in the inventory of tickets, Florence could reasonably have expected, when she made the advances, that repayment would occur shortly; and indeed, the advances were repaid within 2 or 3 years, a relatively short time. Because of these circumstances, together with the characterization of the advances, as "loans" in the books and records, we conclude that they were in fact loans and that the withdrawal by Florence in 1958 was a repayment of such loans and not a dividend.

Since we have decided in this opinion that Barnes overstated its purchases and thereby received additional income during the years 1955 through 1958, we must consider the respondent's further determination that Florence received the amount of the additional income. The respondent contends that Florence received such income as distributions from Barnes, and hence she received income in excess of that reported on her returns.

Florence did not testify and introduced no evidence to refute the respondent's determination in this regard. She relied instead on attempting to prove that the respondent's determinations in regard to Barnes were in error. Florence was the president and sole stockholder of Barnes during the years 1955 through 1958. In view of her failure to rebut the presumption in favor of the respondent's determination relating to her and in view of her relationship to the corporation, we approve that determination.

The respondent also determined that additions to the tax under section 293(a) of the Internal Revenue Code of 1939 and section 6653(a) of the Internal Revenue Code of 1954 for negligence or intentional disregard of rules and regulations were due from Florence for the years 1953 and 1955 through 1958. Florence did not contest these additions; therefore, we must uphold the respondent's determination. *Pearl Zarnow*, 48 T.C. 213 (1967); *David Courtney*, 28 T.C. 658 (1957).

As an alternative, the respondent determined that if Florence did not receive additional income from Barnes, Albert did. The only connection of Albert with Barnes of which we are aware is that he was employed as treasurer. We do not believe that this connection is sufficient to attribute to him, without more, the unreported income of Barnes. Because of this insufficient connection and because of our conclusion that Florence received the additional income from Barnes, we hold that Albert received no additional income from Barnes during the years 1955 through 1958.

In order to reflect computations required by this opinion and the agreement of the parties concerning other adjustments in the notices of deficiency,

Decisions will be entered under Rule 50.

App. 17

In The Tax Court of the United States
* * (Caption—Nos. 1212-64 and 1210-64) * *

DECISION

Pursuant to the opinion of the Court filed December 18, 1967, and incorporating herein the facts recited in the respondent's computation as the findings of the Court, it is

Ordered and Decided: That there are deficiencies in income taxes due from the petitioner for the taxable years 1955, 1956, 1957 and 1958 in the amounts of $27,138.81, $25,427.83, $8,883.60 and $10,239.03, respectively.

Judge.

Entered:

* * *

It is hereby stipulated that the foregoing decision is in accordance with the opinion of the Court and the respondent's computation, and that the Court may enter this decision, without prejudice to the right of either party to contest the correctness of the decision entered herein.

Counsel for Petitioner

Lester R. Uretz
Chief Counsel
Internal Revenue Service

In The Tax Court of the United States
* * (Caption—Nos. 1211-64 and 1210-64) * *

DECISION

Pursuant to the opinion of the Court filed December 18, 1967, and incorporating herein the facts recited in the respondent's computation as the findings of the Court, it is

Ordered and Decided: That there are deficiencies in income taxes due from the petitioners for the taxable years 1955 and 1956 in the amounts of $14.80 and $0.72, respectively;

That there is an overpayment in income tax for the taxable year 1957 in the amount of $86.75, which amount was paid on April 15, 1958, and for which amount a claim for refund could have been filed under the provisions of section 6511(c) of the Internal Revenue Code of 1954, on December 27, 1963, the date of the mailing of the notice of deficiency;

That there is an overpayment in income tax for the taxable year 1958 in the amount of $8.67 which amount was paid on April 15, 1959, and for which amount a claim for refund could have been filed under the provisions of section 6511(c) of the Internal Revenue Code of 1954, on December 27, 1963, the date of the mailing of the notice of deficiency; and

That there are no additions to the taxes due from the petitioners for the taxable years 1955 to 1958, inclusive, under the provisions of section 6653 (a) of the Internal Revenue Code of 1954.

(Signed)   Charles R. Simpson
Judge.

Entered: February 12, 1968.

*   *   *

It is hereby stipulated that the foregoing decision is in accordance with the opinion of the Court and the respondent's computation, and that the Court may enter this decision, without prejudice to the right of either party to contest the correctness of the decision entered herein.

    George D. Crowley
        Counsel for Petitioners
    (Signed)   Lester R. Uretz (CBW)
              Lester R. Uretz
              Chief Counsel
              Internal Revenue Service

IN THE TAX COURT OF THE UNITED STATES
      *   * (Caption—No. 1212-64) * *

DECISION

Pursuant to the opinion of the Court filed December 18, 1967, and incorporating herein the facts recited in the respondent's computation as the findings of the Court, it is

Ordered and Decided: That there are deficiencies in income taxes due the petitioner for the taxable years 1953 1955, 1957 and 1958 in the amounts of $7,162.01, $12,541.27, $7,877.36 and $1,599.17, respectively;

That there is a deficiency in income tax (to be assessed) due from the petitioner for the taxable year 1956 in the amount of $46,643.00;

That there is an addition to the tax due from the petitioner for the taxable year 1953, under the provisions of section 293(a) of the Internal Revenue Code of 1939, in the amount of $358.10; and

That there are additions to the taxes due from the petitioner for the taxable years 1955, 1956, 1957 and 1958 under the provisions of section 6653(a) of the Internal Revenue Code of 1954, in the amounts of $627.06, $2,478.77, $393.87 and $79.96, respectively.

Charles R. Simpson
Judge.

Entered: February 12, 1968.

*   *   *

It is hereby stipulated that the foregoing decision is in accordance with the opinion of the Court and the respondent's computation, and that the Court may enter this decision, without prejudice to the right of either party to contest the correctness of the decision entered herein.

George D. Crowley

    Counsel for Petitioner
Lester R. Uretz
Lester R. Uretz
    Chief Counsel
    Internal Revenue Service

APPENDIX II
Opinion Of The United States Court Of Appeals For The Seventh Circuit

In the
United States Court of Appeals
For the Seventh Circuit

SEPTEMBER TERM, 1968—SEPTEMBER SESSION, 1968

No. 16968

FLORENCE M. BARNES, and BARNES
  THEATRE TICKET SERVICE, INC.,
  an Illinois corporation,
              Petitioner-Appellant,

v.

THE COMMISSIONER OF INTERNAL
  REVENUE,
              Respondent-Appellee.

Appeal from the
United States
Tax Court.

MARCH 5, 1969

Before HASTINGS, *Senior Circuit Judge,* and SWYGERT and CUMMINGS, *Circuit Judges.*

HASTINGS, *Senior Circuit Judge.* The cases of three taxpayers were consolidated for trial in the Tax Court of the United States, Honorable Charles R. Simpson, Judge presiding.

Barnes Theatre Ticket Service, Inc. (Barnes), Docket No. 1210-64.

Albert C. Eckhardt and Cassandra Eckardt (Eckardts), Docket No. 1211-64.

Florence M. Barnes (Florence), Docket No. 1212-64.

The respondent Commissioner of Internal Revenue had asserted deficiencies against the taxpayers in each of the three cases.

Following a trial, the court found and held:[1]

(1)   The issues in Docket No. 1211-64 favorable to the Eckhardts, and the Commissioner has not appealed from this ruling;

(2)   That certain sales made by Barnes to other ticket brokers in the taxable years 1955 through 1958 were "wash sales" which did not result in income to Barnes during those years, and the Commissioner has not appealed from this ruling;

(3)   That the withdrawal of funds by Florence from Barnes in 1958 constituted a repayment of funds previously loaned by her to it and was not taxable to her as a dividend, and the Commissioner has not appealed from this ruling;

(4)   That the Commissioner was correct in finding Barnes had overstated its cost of operations for the taxable years 1955 through 1958 in the following amounts:

---

[1] The thorough and well-considered memorandum findings of fact and opinion of Judge Simpson was filed December 18, 1967, Docket Nos. 1210-64—1212-64, 26 TCM 1290.

COST OF OPERATIONS

Year	Claimed	Allowed	Overstatement Cost of Operation
1955	$569,785.75	$499,010.61	$70,775.14
1956	499,164.30	436,451.28	62,713.02
1957	391,912.95	370,077.06	21,835.89
1958	475,372.89	460,929.65	14,443.24

And, that Florence realized additional taxable income from Barnes in the years 1955 through 1958 in amounts corresponding to the overstated costs of operation disallowed to Barnes.

Barnes and Florence now file their joint petition for review.

The contested issues on review may be generally stated as (1) whether the Tax Court correctly held that Barnes failed to sustain its burden of showing that its costs of operations exceeded the amounts allowed by the Commissioner; and (2) whether the Tax Court correctly held that Florence, president and sole shareholder of Barnes, had taxable income (constructive dividends) to the extent that Barnes overstated its cost of operations.

Based on our examination of the record, we shall summarize the facts relevant to this review.

During the taxable years in question, Florence was the president of and sole shareholder in Barnes, an Illinois corporation, whose principal office was located in the Palmer House Hotel in downtown Chicago.

Barnes, engaging in the ticket brokerage business, purchased tickets of admission to sundry entertainment events and then resold them at charges in excess of established box office prices. The tickets were resold from a counter adjacent to the corporate offices in the Palmer House Hotel and from 14 other stands located in hotels and private clubs in the Chicago area.

Control over both the purchase and the resale of tickets was maintained by Barnes' central office in the Palmer House.

Barnes secured tickets for resale from many different sources. It purchased them from box offices of various theaters and sporting arenas and from persons or organizations engaged in the production of treatrical performances and sporting events; Barnes also bought tickets via mail orders and from people not regularly engaged in the ticket vending business.

Under a working arrangement with the box office personnel of various theatres and sporting arenas, choice tickets of admission for different Chicago attractions were forwarded to Barnes' office at the Palmer House. Included with the tickets from each box office was a slip of paper which set forth the cost per ticket, the number of tickets purchased, and the amount of premium, if any, over the box office price paid by Barnes. Barnes' bookkeeper, Anne Magner, recorded in the regular course of business *some* of the information found on these slips of paper; thereafter, Miss Magner destroyed the box office slips. Under this arrangement, Barnes was permitted to return, prior to a performance or event, unsold tickets to the appropriate box office for full refund of the purchase price.

Barnes maintained close daily control over the sale of tickets by requiring each of its vending stands to send the main office proceeds from each day's sales, together with a sheet indicating the date, the number of tickets sold by the stand, the number of tickets being returned, the amount of money received, the customer's name, the names of the theaters to which the tickets applied, and an inventory of tickets. The accompanying sheets contained neither a designation as to the cost of the tickets to Barnes nor a figure indicating the premium paid for the tickets, if any, over established box office prices. The daily proceeds were checked against these sheets and then entered into the cash receipt book. Currency proceeds from sales were either deposited in Barnes' bank account or placed in the office safe to serve as operating capital. Check proceeds were deposited in Barnes' bank account.

Miss Magner summarized monthly the daily stand reports and drew up quarterly summaries which were utilized in the preparation of Barnes' federal excise tax return. The quarterly sales recaps did not, however, reflect a complete record of all Barnes' ticket sales; the quarterly figures excluded sales made at box office prices and for charitable functions and included only those sales on which an excise tax was due. The type of tickets sold, the box office price of the tickets and Barnes' selling price can be determined from these quarterly sales recaps.

Although Barnes' cash receipts book and cash disbursements book (Exhibits 15 and 16) are not in the record before us, we assume that the Tax Court's conclusions with respect to these books are correct since neither party disputes those findings upon appeal.

In 1955, the cash receipts book reveals total cash purchases by Barnes on a per week per theater basis. For the later taxable years in question, the cash receipts book indicates cash purchases for periods varying from one to several weeks and is generally without entries showing the names of the theaters and persons from whom tickets were purchased, the dates of the purchases, and the amounts paid for particular tickets or bundles of tickets.

While the majority of the ticket purchases by Barnes were cash transactions, some were paid for by check. All purchases by check for the year 1955 through 1958 were recorded in the cash disbursements books.

Based essentially on these faces, the Tax Court upheld the Commissioner's determination that the cost of operation alleged by Barnes Theatre Service, Inc. was overstated during the years 1955 through 1958 and that the amount of such overstatement constituted additional income to Mrs. Barnes. These holdings were premised on the court's conclusion that the petitioners failed to overcome the presumption of correctness which normally attaches to Internal Revenue determinations of this nature.

To hurdle the presumption obstacle, the tax court suggested that the taxpayer show "* * * that the asserted deficiency was computed in an improper manner or * * * [show] that its books and records are adequate and accurately reflect its income, or * * * [produce] a combination of such evidence."

In this case, the Tax Court specifically found that Barnes' books and records failed to adequately and reliably reflect costs of operation; and that Barnes adduced no evidence with respect to the propriety of the computation of the asserted deficiency.

Taxpayers contend that the statutory notices of deficiency were so incomplete that the presumption of correctness should not attach to the determination. Further, that since the statutory notices neglected to state the basis for the deficiency determination the action of the Commissioner was arbitrary and therefore invalid. We disagree with taxpayers on both contentions.

We are of the opinion that the notice of deficiency complies with the statute, Section 6212(a) of the 1954 Code, which provides in general that "If the Secretary or his delegate determines that there is a deficiency in respect of any tax * * *, he is authorized to send notice of such deficiency to the taxpayer by certified mail or registered mail." Int. Rev. Code of 1954, § 6212. *Commissioner of Internal Revenue v. Forest Glen C. Co.,* 7 Cir., 98 F. 2d 968, 971 (1938), cert. denied, 306 U.S. 638.

Further, it seems clear that the Commissioner's notice of deficiency is not invalidated because it contains no particulars or explanations concerning how the alleged deficiencies were determined. *Commissioner of Internal Revenue v. Stewart,* 6 Cir., 186 F.2d 239, 242 (1951).

It was cogently stated in *Olsen v. Helvering,* 2 Cir., 88 F. 2d 650, 651 (1937) that "the notice is only to advise the person who is to pay the deficiency that the Commissioner means to assess him; anything that does this unequivocally is good enough."

As Judge Simpson noted in 26 TCM at 1293: "In so holding, we are not approving of the deficiency; we are merely saying that the notice of deficiency is sufficient to raise the presumption of correctness and to place the burden of proof on the petitioners."

We find no prejudice to taxpayers resulting from the form of the statutory notices. The contentions urged and won on other issues are indicative that the taxpayers were fully informed of the Commissioner's actions.

It is axiomatic that unless otherwise provided by statute the Commissioner's tax deficiency determinations are to be presumed correct. The presumption is procedural and transfers to the taxpayer the burden of going forward with the evidence to show that the Commissioner's determination is incorrect. Tax Court Rule 32, 26 U.S.C.A. § 7453; *Foster* v. *C.I.R.*, 4 Cir., 391 F. 2d 727, 735 (1968); *Stout* v. *C.I.R.*, 4 Cir., 273 F. 2d 345, 350 (1959); *Cohen* v. *C.I.R.*, 9 Cir., 266 F. 2d 5, 11 (1959); *Zeddies* v. *C.I.R.*, 7 Cir., 264 F. 2d 120, 126 (1959). See 9 Mertens, Law of Federal Income Taxation § 50.61. To overcome the presumption, it is not incumbent on the taxpayer to prove he owes nothing or to show the correct amount which he might owe. *Helvering* v. *Taylor*, 293 U.S. 507, 514 (1935); *United States* v. *Hover*, 9 Cir., 268 F. 2d 657, 665 (1959). It is equally true that the Commissioner's determination is invalid when it is shown to be arbitrary or capricious. *Helvering* v. *Taylor, supra; Cohen* v. *C.I.R., supra* at 11; 9 Mertens *supra* at § 50.65.

The critical question then arises, as stated by the Tax Court, whether taxpayers adduced sufficient evidence showing that the asserted deficiencies were computed in an improper manner or by showing that its books and records adequately and accurately reflected its income, or by producing a combination of such evidence.

In a careful and detailed analysis of the evidence presented by taxpayers, the court found that Barnes had failed to show "that its books and records accurately reflect its costs of operation." 26 TCM at 1294. We agree. This conclusion is buttressed by the failure of Florence to testify or to explain her admissions to the Commissioner's agent that the records of Barnes did not reflect the true cost of the tickets. She was present during the hearing.

It is apparent that while Barnes' books and records seem quite complete in recording its income, the failure lies in the incomplete information used to record the cost of the tickets. Invoices were destroyed; there was a lack of substantiation of the figures appearing in the recaps; and there was no identification of any person or theater to whom premium prices were paid for tickets.

In addition to the failure of the books and records to substantiate the cost of tickets, Florence admitted to Special Agent Shadduck that the books were inaccurate and did not reflect the true cost of the tickets and that expenses other than the purchase of tickets were included on the recap sheets. Some of these extra expenses were payments to legislators as "lobbying" expenses. When asked for further identification of her sources of tickets, Florence replied, "If I tell you, I will be out of business, because the source of my tickets will dry out." For whatever reasons she may have had, Florence did not testify.

We agree with Judge Simpson's observation: "Finally, a very dark cloud is cast on the reliability of the cost information in the books by statements which Florence made to the agent of respondent during the investigation of the tax liabilities of Barnes." We further agree that taxpayers' objections to the admission of this testimony were properly denied. 26 TCM at 1294.

Taxpayers contend with much force that the Commissioner erred in not introducing the testimony of Agent George Mowdry at the trial. It is conceded that Mowdry was primarily responsible for the income tax investigation of Barnes and prepared the assessment of deficiencies asserted in the notices. It was also suggested during the trial that the court would "have to wait until Mr. Mowdry is on the stand to attempt to establish [Barnes' income tax deficiency].'' Mowdry did not testify and was not called to the stand by either party. The manner in which the alleged overstatement in costs was computed was not shown.

While the overall approach of the Internal Revenue Service to this case has been a source of vexation to the taxpayers and has made the decision in this case difficult, we have no doubt that if Barnes' books and records had been shown to be accurate and reliable[2] and had Florence testified, then without the testimony of Agent Mowdry we would be compelled to reverse and find for taxpayers.

However, in the absence of such showing by the taxpayers and in light of the record in this case, we cannot say that such adverse findings by the Tax Court are clearly erroneous. *Banks* v. *C.I.R.*, 8 Cir., 322 F. 2d 530, 537 (1963). We have found no authority justifying a departure from the well-established rule of presumption of correctness, under the findings in this case.

We, therefore, conclude and hold that the evidence adduced by taxpayers was not sufficient to overcome the presumption of correctness.

We have carefully read the entire record in this case and authorities cited by both parties. Contentions not specifically mentioned here are found to be without merit.

---

[2] Pursuant to § 6001 of the Internal Revenue Code of 1954, Federal Tax Regulation 1.6001-1 provides that a taxpayer "shall keep such permanent books of account or records, * * * as are sufficient to establish the amount of gross income, deductions, credits, or other matters required to be shown by such person in any return of such tax or information."

For the foregoing reasons, the petition for review is denied and the decisions of the Tax Court under review are affirmed.

PETITION DENIED.

DECISIONS AFFIRMED.

SWYGERT, *Circuit Judge,* dissenting.

I dissent for two reasons. First, despite the majority's statement that "We have found no authority justifying a departure from the well-established rule of presumption of correctness," I believe that under the circumstances here presented the weight accorded by the Tax Court to the Commissioner's deficiency notice was erroneous. Secondly, I am of the opinion that the majority's position, if logically extended, could lead in the future to an unfortunate level of high-handedness on the part of the Commissioner.

My difficulty with the majority's opinion begins with what I believe to be a mistaken statement of the contested issue. The real question presented by this case is what effect should be given by the Tax Court to the Commissioner's notice of deficiency in a situation where the taxpayer asserts that the notice is incomplete and arbitrary. As the majority recognizes it is settled that as a general rule a presumption of correctness attaches to the Commissioner's deficiency notice. It is my view that, although this presumtion is one which places on the taxpayer the burden of going forward with evidence, by no stretch of the imagination can it be the basis of a judgment favorable to the Commissioner when the notice is arbitrary, even if the taxpayer's books cannot disprove every possible theory of taxation.

Stated simply, the majority's position is that once the Commissioner's deficiency notice is introduced into evidence and the production burden consequently moves to the taxpayer, he can shift this burden back to the Commissioner only when his books can conclusively disprove the asserted deficiency. This construction oversimplifies the functioning of the correctness presumption. Although I agree that if at trial the taxpayer offers *no* evidence, the Commissioner's deficiency notice is sufficient evidence to find in his favor, I do not believe that this Commissioner-wins rule should operate if the taxpayer produces competent evidence on the issue of the arbitrariness of the asserted deficiency. If the taxpayer offers some competent evidence on this point, then the question of the existence of a deficiency must be decided on all the evidence submitted at the trial.

The law is clear that the presumption of correctness which ordinarily attaches to the action of the Commissioner vanishes if his action is arbitrary. *Helvering v. Taylor,* 293 U.S. 507 (1935). See also *Gasper v. Commissioner,* 225 F.2d 284 (6th Cir. 1955); *Welch v. Commissioner,* 297 F.2d 309 (4th Cir. 1961). The deficiency notice in the instant case contained the asserted tax deficiencies which were based on the alleged overstated costs of the taxpayers' operations, spelled out to the penny. This is not a case where the Commissioner with proper candor acknowledges that because of a taxpayer's inadequate records an admittedly arbitrary deficiency figure has been chosen. What happened here was that after introduction of the deficiency notice with its apparently meticulously calculated figures, the taxpayers sought through the introduction of their books and records to establish the fact not only that they owed no additional tax, but also to demonstrate that the Commissioner's deficiency notice had no ascertainable empirical basis. The Commissioner offered no evidence to rebut the taxpayers' contention. In effect, what the taxpayers sought to do was to elicit from the Commissioner precisely what costs of operation he concluded they had erroneously included in their tax computations. The taxpayers' request to know what cost items were being disallowed was surely reasonable.

Nonetheless, the Tax Court disregarded the taxpayers' attack on the deficiency notice and invoked the correctness presumption on the ground that the taxpayers had failed to show that their books and records accurately reflected the ticket agency's cost of operation. Likewise, this court holds that because the taxpayers' books were not suitable to disprove all the Commissioner's theories of cost and taxation, the taxpayers cannot attack the arbitrariness of the Commissioner's deficiency notice. This approach is tantamount to saying that a taxpayer whose books are not one hundred per cent accurate has no standing to challenge or question a deficiency notice, however arbitrary.

Nothing in the prior case law justifies a holding that the maintenance of perfect account books is a prerequisite to the taxpayer's right to challenge the arbitrariness of a deficiency notice. In my opinion a court should not reach the question of the quality of a taxpayer's books if the taxpayer asserts and demonstrates that the Commissioner's deficiency is arbitrary. As the Sixth Circuit said in *Durkee* v. *Commissioner,* 162 F.2d 184, 187 (6th Cir. 1947): "But where it is apparent from the record that the Commissioner's determination is arbitrary and excessive, the taxpayer is not required to establish the correct amount that lawfully might be charged against him, and he is not required to pay a tax that he obviously does not owe. In proceedings before the Tax Court . . . it is sufficient to show that the Commissioner's determination is invalid. Upon such a showing the case should be remanded to the Tax Court for further hearings on the point involved." Such an approach should be followed here. In the instant case, the Commissioner had an opportunity to offer evidence as to the basis, if any, of his deficiency assessment. Agent George Mowdry, who conducted the special income tax investigation into the Barnes' tax matter, was never called to the stand by the Commissioner to explain how the deficiency had been computed.

In reality the Tax Court by casting doubt on the reliability of the taxpayers' evidence ruled that they had produced no evidence at all. This conclusion was unwarranted. Once competent evidence is proffered which indicates the incompleteness or arbitrariness of the deficiency notice, the presumption of correctness disappears regardless of the absolute reliability of the taxpayer's evidence. At this point the production burden shifts back to the Commissioner to show how he arrived at his determination. The Commissioner cannot avoid his burden by merely discrediting the taxpayer's evidence. In an analogous factual situation, this court said: "The disbelief of . . . testimony [of the witness] cannot support an affirmative finding that the reverse of his testimony is true, that is, it cannot supply a want of proof." *Bankers Life and Casualty Co.* v. *Guarantee Reserve Life Ins. Co.,* 365 F.2d 28, 34 (7th Cir. 1966), *cert. denied,* 386 U.S. 913 (1967). Similarly here, it does not follow that because the taxpayers' books cannot disprove the theory of taxation selected by the Commissioner, the Commissioner's assessment is correct and cannot be shown to be arbitrary.

Additionally, I am concerned with what the majority's decision might permit the Commissioner to do with future taxpayers. If the Commissioner knows that a particular taxpayer's books and records are not any more accurate or all encompassing than those kept by the Barnes' ticket agency, as a result of our decision, there is nothing to prevent the Commissioner from selecting an arbitrary figure, putting it in a tax deficiency notice, and then proceeding to enforce the deficiency. Our decision would allow the Commissioner to prevail, despite the completely arbitrary nature of his assessment, because the taxpayer's insufficient books would preclude him from attacking the deficiency. On account of his imperfect bookkeeping, a taxpayer would be deprived of his standing just as the taxpayers here were unable to pierce the veil of the correctness presumption in the instant case.

A true Copy:

Teste:

Clerk of the United States Court of Appeals for the Seventh Circuit.

APPENDIX III
Order Denying Petition For Rehearing En Banc

UNITED STATES COURT OF APPEALS

For the Seventh Circuit
Chicago, Illinois 60604

Thursday, April 10, 1969

Before

Hon. Latham Castle, *Chief Judge*

Hon. John S. Hastings, *Senior Circuit Judge*

Hon. Roger J. Kiley, *Circuit Judge*

Hon. Luther M. Swygert, *Circuit Judge*

Hon. Thomas E. Fairchild, *Circuit Judge*

Hon. Walter J. Cummings, *Circuit Judge*

Hon. Otto Kerner, *Circuit Judge*

BARNES THEATRE TICKET SERVICE, INC.,
FLORENCE M. BARNES,
Petitioners,
No. 16968   vs.
COMMISSIONER OF INTERNAL REVENUE,
Respondent.

Petition for review of a decision of the Tax Court of the United States

IT IS ORDERED by the Court that the petition of the petitioners for a rehearing *en banc* of the above entitled cause be, and the same is hereby DENIED.

(Circuit Judges Swygert and Kerner voted to grant the petition for rehearing *en banc*.)

APPENDIX IV

Order Recalling And Staying Mandate Of The United States Court Of Appeals For The Seventh Circuit

UNITED STATES COURT OF APPEALS
For the Seventh Circuit
Chicago, Illinois 60604

Monday, May 12, 1969

Before

Hon. John S. Hastings, *Sr. Circuit Judge*

Barnes Theatre Ticket Service, Inc., Florence M. Barnes, *Petitioners,* No. 16968 vs. Commissioner of Internal Revenue, *Respondent.*	Petition for review from an order from the Tax Court of the United States

On consideration of the motion and affidavit of counsel for petitioner for a stay of mandate, such motion being treated by this Court as a motion for recall and stay of mandate since this Court's mandate to the Tax Court of the United States has previously been issued on April 23, 1969,

IT IS ORDERED that the mandate of this Court be and the same is hereby recalled, and upon recall, it be stayed for a period of thirty (30) days in accordance with the provisions of Rule 41(b) of the Federal Rules of Appellate Procedure.

APPENDIX V

**Order Staying Mandate Of The United States Court of
Appeals For The Seventh Circuit**

UNITED STATES COURT OF APPEALS
For the Seventh Circuit
Chicago, Illinois 60604

Wednesday, June 11, 1969

Before

Hon. John S. Hastings, *Senior Circuit Judge*

Barnes Theatre Ticket Service, Inc.,
    Florence M. Barnes,
          Petitioners-Appellants,
No. 16968   vs.
Commissioner of Internal Revenue,
         Respondent-Appellee.

Petition for review of a decision of the Tax Court of the United States

On consideration of the motion and affidavit of counsel for petitioner-appellant,

IT IS ORDERED that the issuance of the mandate of this Court be further stayed to July 9, 1969, in accordance with the provisions of Rule 41 of the Federal Rules of Appellate Procedure.

APPENDIX VI

Constitutional Provisions And Statutes Involved

FIFTH AMENDMENT TO THE CONSTITUTION OF THE UNITED STATES

No person shall be held to answer for a capital, or otherwise infamous crime, unless on a presentment or indictment of a Grand Jury, except in cases arising in the land or naval forces, or in the Militia, when in actual service in time of War or public danger; nor shall any person be subject for the same offense to be twice put in jeopardy of life or limb; nor shall be compelled in any criminal case to be a witness against himself, nor be deprived of life, liberty or property, without due process of law; nor shall private property be taken for public use, without just compensation.

TITLE 26 UNITED STATES CODE SECTION 6212(a)-

(a) IN GENERAL — If the Secretary or his delegate determines that there is a deficiency in respect of any tax imposed by subtitles A or B, he is authorized to send notice of such deficiency to the taxpayer by certified mail or registered mail.

TAX COURT RULES OF PRACTICE, RULE 32

The burden of proof shall be upon the petitioner, except as otherwise provided by statute, and except that in respect of any new matter pleaded in his answer, it shall be upon the respondent.

(The Tax Court Rules follow Title 26, United States Code, Section 7453).

TITLE 26 UNITED STATES CODE SECTION 7453

The proceedings of the Tax Court and its divisions shall be conducted in accordance with such rules of practice and procedure (other than rules of evidence) as the Tax Court may prescribe and in accordance with the rules of evidence applicable in trials without a jury in the United States District Court of the District of Columbia.

APPENDIX VII

Notice of Deficiency

(Seal)

U. S. TREASURY DEPARTMENT
Internal Revenue Service
Regional Commissioner
Appellate Division
Post Office Box FF
Chicago, Illinois 60690
Dec. 27, 1963

In Reply Refer to
ARC:AP:CHI:RFS:GGO

Taxable year Ended	Deficiency
Dec.31,1955	$32,763.18
Dec.31,1956	33,295.98
Dec.31,1957	11,175.89
Dec.31,1958	11,428.55

Barnes Theatre Ticket Service, Inc.
17 East Monroe Street
Chicago 3, Illinois

Gentlemen:

In accordance with the provisions of existing internal revenue laws, notice is given that the determination of your income tax liability for the above-noted taxable year(s) discloses a deficiency (or deficiencies) in the amount(s) shown above. The attached statement shows the computation of the deficiency or deficiencies.

IF YOU AGREE to this determination, please sign the enclosed agreement, Form 870, and return it promptly to this office. An addressed envelope is enclosed for this purpose. The signing and filing of this agreement will permit an early assessment of the deficiency or deficiencies and will limit the accumulation of interest.

App. 41

IF YOU DO NOT AGREE, and do not sign and return
the enclosed form, the deficiency or deficiencies will be
assessed for collection, as required by law, upon the expiration of ninety days from the date of this letter, unless
within that time you contest this determination in the Tax
Court of the United States by filing a petition with that
Court in accordance with its rules, a copy of which may
be obtained by writing to its Clerk, Box 70, Washington
4, D.C.

Very truly yours,

Mortimer M. Caplin
Commissioner
By (Signed) Harold Aronson
Associate Chief
Appellate Division, Chicago Region

Enclosures —
Statement
Agreement, Form 870
Addressed envelope
ARC:AP:CHI:RFS:GGO

STATEMENT

Barnes Theatre Ticket Service, Inc.
17 East Monroe Street
Chicago 3, Illinois

Year	Deficiency
1955	$32,763.18
1956	33,295.98
1957	11,175.89
1958	11,428.55
Total	$88,663.60

In making this determination of your income tax liability, careful consideration has been given to your protest dated April 30, 1962, in regard to the District Director's preliminary determination of your tax liability and to the statements made at the conferences held on June 7 and October 19, 1962, July 9, July 17 and August 28, 1963.

It is determined that you overstated your cost of operations in the amounts of $70,775.14, $62,713.02, $21,835.89 and $14,443.24 for the years 1955, 1956, 1957 and 1958, respectively, since you failed to substantiate that your aggregate cost of operations exceeded amounts allowed in the following tabulation:

COST OF OPERATIONS

Year	Claimed	Allowed	Overstatement Cost of Operation
1955	$569,785.75	$499,010.61	$70,775.14
1956	499,164.30	436,451.28	62,713.02
1957	391,912.95	370,077.06	21,835.89
1958	475,372.89	460,929.65	14,443.24

Copies of this letter and statement have been mailed to your representative, Mr. George D. Crowley, 135 South LaSalle Street, Chicago 3, Illinois, in accordance with the authority contained in the power of attorney executed by you and on file with the Internal Revenue Service.

Taxable Year Ended December 31, 1955

ADJUSTMENTS TO INCOME

Taxable income (loss) shown on return $(9,123.38)
Additional income and unallowable deductions:

(a)	Cost of operations	70,775.14
(b)	Income from broker transactions	9,700.91
(c)	Other deductions	1,182.02
(d)	Depreciation	1,048.35

Taxable income as adjusted $73,583.04

EXPLANATION OF ADJUSTMENTS

(a) thru (d) For explanation of these adjustments, see the preliminary portion of this statement.

COMPUTATION OF TAX

Taxable income as adjusted	$73,583.04

Income tax ($73,583.04 @ 52% less $5,500.00)	$32,763.18
Tax shown on return, # CN 719	None

Deficiency	$32,763.18

Taxable Year Ended December 31, 1956

ADJUSTMENTS TO INCOME

Taxable income (loss) shown on return	$(4,387.93)

Additional income and unallowable deductions:

(a) Cost of operations	62,713.02
(b) Income from broker transactions	13,979.55
(c) Other deductions	1,254.66
(d) Depreciation	1,048.35

Taxable income as adjusted	$74,607.65

EXPLANATION OF ADJUSTMENTS

(a) thru (d) For explanation of these adjustments, see the preliminary portion of this statement.

COMPUTATION OF TAX

Taxable income as adjusted	$74,607.65

Income tax ($74,607.65 @ 52% less $5,500.00)	$33,295.98
Tax shown on return, #CN 201177	None

Deficiency	$33,295.98

Taxable Year Ended December 31, 1957

ADJUSTMENTS TO INCOME

Taxable income as reflected on return	$ None
Additional income and unallowable deductions:	
(a) Cost of operations	21,835.89
(b) Income from broker transactions	3,176.11
(c) Other deductions	1,328.59
(d) Depreciation	1,135.73
(e) Net operating loss deduction	4,592.70
Taxable income as adjusted	$32,069.02

EXPLANATION OF ADJUSTMENTS

(a) thru(e) For explanation of these adjustments, see the preliminary portion of this statement.

COMPUTATION OF TAX

Taxable income as adjusted	$32,069.02
Income tax ($32,069.02 @ 52% less $5,500.00)	$11,175.89
Tax shown on return, # CN 202832	None
Deficiency	$11,175.89

Taxable Year Ended December 31, 1958

ADJUSTMENTS TO INCOME

Taxable income shown on return	$23,727.20
Additional income and unallowable deductions:	
(a) Cost of operations	14,443.24
(b) Income from broker transactions	1,415.63
(c) Other deductions	1,743.80
(d) Net operating loss deduction	4,888.41
Taxable income as adjusted	$46,278.28

EXPLANATION OF ADJUSTMENTS

(a) thru (d) For explanation of these adjustments, see the preliminary portion of this statement.

COMPUTATION OF TAX

Taxable income as adjusted	$46,278.28
Income tax ($46,278.28 @ 52% less $5,500.00)	$18,564.71
Tax shown on return, # CF 202004	7,136.16
Deficiency	$11,428.55

APPENDIX VIII

Statutory Basis For Tax Jurisdiction

TITLE 26 UNITED STATES CODE SECTION 7442

The Tax Court and its divisions shall have such jurisdiction as is conferred on them by this title, by chapters 1, 2, 3, and 4 of the Internal Revenue Code of 1939, by title II and title III of the Revenue Act of 1926 (44 Stat. 10-87), or by the laws enacted subsequent to February 26, 1926.

TITLE 26 UNITED STATES CODE SECTION 6213(a)

(a) Time For Filing Petition And Restriction On Assessment.—Within 90 days, or 150 days if the notice is addressed to a person outside the States of the Union and the District of Columbia, after the notice of deficiency authorized in section 6212 is mailed (not counting Saturday, Sunday, or a legal holiday in the District of Columbia as the last day), the taxpayer may file a petition with the Tax Court for a redetermination of the deficiency. Except as otherwise provided in section 6861 no assessment of a deficiency in respect of any tax imposed by subtitle A or B and no levy or proceeding in court for its collection shall be made, begun, or prosecuted until such notice has been mailed to the taxpayer, nor until the expiration of such 90-day or 150-day period, as the case may be, nor, if a petition has been filed with the Tax Court, until the decision of the Tax Court has become final. Notwithstanding the provisions of section 7421(a), the making of such assessment or the beginning of such proceeding or levy during the time such prohibition is in force may be enjoined by a proceeding in the proper court.

No. 314

$\mathfrak{In}$ the $\mathfrak{Supreme}$ $\mathfrak{Court}$ of the $\mathfrak{United}$ $\mathfrak{States}$

OCTOBER TERM, 1969

FLORENCE M. BARNES AND BARNES THEATRE TICKET
SERVICE, INC., PETITIONERS

v.

COMMISSIONER OF INTERNAL REVENUE

*ON PETITION FOR A WRIT OF CERTIORARI TO THE UNITED
STATES COURT OF APPEALS FOR THE SEVENTH CIRCUIT*

BRIEF FOR THE UNITED STATES IN OPPOSITION

ERWIN N. GRISWOLD,
Solicitor General.
JOHNNIE M. WALTERS,
Assistant Attorney General.
WILLIAM A. FRIEDLANDER,
STEPHEN H. HUTZELMAN,
Attorneys,
Department of Justice,
Washington, D.C. 20530.

In the Supreme Court of the United States

No. 314

FLORENCE M. BARNES AND BARNES THEATRE TICKET
SERVICE, INC., PETITIONERS

v.

COMMISSIONER OF INTERNAL REVENUE

*ON PETITION FOR A WRIT OF CERTIORARI TO THE UNITED
STATES COURT OF APPEALS FOR THE SEVENTH CIRCUIT*

BRIEF FOR THE UNITED STATES IN OPPOSITION

OPINIONS BELOW

The Memorandum Findings of Fact and Opinion of
the Tax Court (R. 151–167;[1] Pet. App. 1–16) are not
officially reported. The opinion of the court of appeals
(Pet. App. 21–35) is reported at 408 F. 2d 65.

JURISDICTION

The judgment of the court of appeals was entered
on March 5, 1969. A petition for rehearing en banc
was denied on April 10, 1969 (Pet. App. 36). The
petition for a writ of certiorari was filed on July 5,

---

[1] "R." refers to the appendix to petitioners' brief in the court
of appeals. "Supp. R." refers to the appendix to respondent's
brief in the court of appeals.

(1)

1969. The jurisdiction of this Court is invoked under 28 U.S.C. 1254(1).

QUESTION PRESENTED

Whether the application of the usual presumption of correctness to a federal tax deficiency notice constituted a denial of due process where the notice failed to state with particularity how the deficiency had been computed and the taxpayers failed to establish either that the Commissioner's determination was erroneous or that their books and records adequately reflected income.

STATUTE INVOLVED

Internal Revenue Code of 1954:

SEC. 6212. NOTICE OF DEFICIENCY.

(a) [as amended by Sec. 89(b), Technical Amendments Act of 1958, P.L. 85-866, 72 Stat. 1665-1666]. *In General.*—If the Secretary or his delegate determines that there is a deficiency in respect of any tax imposed by subtitles A or B, he is authorized to send notice of such deficiency to the taxpayer by certified mail or registered mail.

*   *   *   *   *

[26 U.S.C. 6212.]

STATEMENT

Petitioner Florence M. Barnes (Florence) has been president and sole shareholder of petitioner Barnes Theatre Ticket Service, Inc., of Chicago, Illinois (Barnes), since its incorporation in 1947. Barnes is a "ticket broker" which resells tickets of admission to theatres and other places of amusement at charges greater than box office prices. (Pet. App. 3-4.)

The Commissioner determined that payments by Barnes to Florence in 1958 were dividends and that Barnes understated its gross income from sales to other brokers for 1955 through 1958. The Tax Court ruled in favor of petitioners on these issues. (Pet. App. 11–16.) The Commissioner also determined that Barnes did not adequately substantiate its costs of operation. He disallowed a portion of the cost of tickets sold claimed by Barnes but did not state the manner in which the deficiency had been computed in his deficiency notice. (Pet. App. 6–7; R. 23.) [2] At trial, petitioners failed to show either that the asserted deficiency was computed in an improper manner or that their books and records adequately reflected the cost of tickets sold. The Tax Court accordingly held that petitioners had failed to overcome the presumption of correctness normally attaching to the Commissioner's determination and sustained that determination. (Pet. App. 7–12.) The court of appeals affirmed. (Pet. App. 21–31.)

ARGUMENT

The decision below, affirming that of the Tax Court with respect to Barnes' overstatement of its cost of

---

[2] The Tax Court also found (Pet. App. 15–16) that, growing out of its holding of Barnes' overstated cost of sales and consequent understatment of taxable income, Florence received additional dividend income during the years 1955 through 1958 as distributions from Barnes. Petitioners introduced no evidence to refute the Commissioner's determination in this regard and instead attempted to prove the determination as to Barnes in error. The Tax Court held that Florence failed to overcome the presumption of correctness in favor of the determination and the Court of Appeals affirmed. (Pet. App. 31.)

tickets sold, is correct, and there is no conflict of decisions or other occasion for further review.

1. In lieu of an effort to overcome the presumption of correctness attaching to the Commissioner's determination, petitioners claim they were denied due process because the statutory notice of deficiency did not state the manner in which the deficiency had been computed. They further claim they were denied due process because the presumption of correctness procedurally required them to go forward with the evidence to show that the Commissioner's determination was erroneous or that their books and records properly reflected the cost of tickets sold. Neither of these contentions has merit.

Section 6212(a) of the Internal Revenue Code of 1954, *supra*, p. 2, requires no special form for a statutory notice of deficiency. *Commissioner v. Forest Glen C. Co.*, 98 F. 2d 968, 971 (C.A. 7). So long as the notice advises the person who is to pay of the amount of the deficiency proposed, it is valid and sufficient to raise the presumption of correctness and to place the burden of proof on the taxpayer. *Commissioner v. Stewart*, 186 F. 2d 239 (C.A. 6); *Olsen v. Helvering*, 88 F. 2d 650 (C.A. 2). No contrary authority is cited and no such authority exists.

Petitioners were not prejudiced by the form of the deficiency notice. As the court of appeals recognized (Pet. App. 27), petitioners' ability to settle many issues before trial (R. 29–31) and to prevail on two major issues at trial (Pet. App. 11–16), as well as the analysis of the issues reflected in their petition and opening statement to the Tax Court (R. 19; Supp.

R. 4–5), indicate a complete awareness of the various questions involved.[3]

Nor were petitioners prejudiced because the burden of going forward with the evidence was imposed upon them. Petitioners had every opportunity to rebut the presumption of correctness attaching to the Commissioner's determination by presenting competent and credible evidence to the trier of fact on the basis of which the trier could find facts inconsistent with the Commissioner's determination. This could be done by showing that the Commissioner's determination was erroneous or that their books and records adequately reflected income, or by a combination of such evidence. (Pet. App. 28.) The Tax Court held (Pet. App. 9) that petitioners adduced no evidence as to the manner in which the Commissioner computed the deficiency.

Petitioners sought to establish the required inconsistent facts by offering corporate books and records as purported evidence that the claimed costs of tickets sold were correct. The books and records, however, contained only summary figures as to ticket costs, and the underlying original documents had been destroyed

---

[3] With respect to the matter of due process, petitioners do not claim that they were not well aware, by the time of trial, of the fact that their records as to ticket purchase costs were in issue and of how the Commissioner had recomputed those costs. In his opening statement before the Tax Court (Supp. R. 4), counsel for taxpayers, Mr. Crowley, acknowledged awareness that "the prime issue is a disallowance of a portion of the cost of goods sold for alleged lack of substantiation." Moreover, if petitioners felt that they were handicapped by the form of notice, they had the opportunity under Rule 17(c), Rules of Practice, Tax Court of the United States (Rev. 1958, 1968 ed.) to file a motion for a more definite statement. This they failed to do.

(R. 155), thus making it impossible to verify the claimed ticket costs. In addition, the Tax Court considered statements by Florence, in the nature of admissions, that the books and records did not reflect the true cost of tickets and that entries so labeled actually included other types of expenditures (Pet. App. 10–11; Supp. R. 11–23). On this record, the Tax Court concluded (Pet. App. 11–12) that petitioners' books and records were unreliable and were not, therefore, competent to overcome the Commissioner's determination.

It follows that there was no deprivation of due process by reason of the imposition of the burden of proof. Petitioners were unable to overcome the presumption of correctness solely because of their own failure to keep adequate books and records of ticket costs as required by Section 6001 of the 1954 Code. They attempt here, as they attempted below, to take advantage of their own default and of evidentiary gaps resulting from the lack of proper records. Since the Tax Court found, however, that petitioners' books and records were unreliable, and since this finding is not clearly erroneous, there is no basis for further review of the court of appeals' affirmance of the Tax Court decision. *Commissioner* v. *Duberstein*, 363 U.S. 278, 291.

2. The decision below is not in conflict with *Helvering* v. *Taylor*, 293 U.S. 507. *Taylor* held that the Commissioner's determination will not be sustained where it is "shown" (293 U.S. 514) that the determination is arbitrary and excessive. As we have demonstrated, no such showing was made here. Moreover, both the

Tax Court and the court of appeals carefully noted, in accordance with the rule of the *Taylor* case (Pet. App. 9, 28), that petitioners were not required to prove the correct amount of tax liability or that there was no such liability. Contrary to petitioners' assertion, therefore, the court of appeals' decision is completely consistent with the holding in *Taylor* and does not sanction an arbitrary determination by the Commissioner.

CONCLUSION

The petition for a writ of certiorari should be denied.

Respectfully submitted.

> ERWIN N. GRISWOLD,
> *Solicitor General.*
> JOHNNIE M. WALTERS,
> *Assistant Attorney General.*
> WILLIAM A. FRIEDLANDER,
> STEPHEN H. HUTZELMAN,
> *Attorneys.*

AUGUST 1969.

Lightning Source UK Ltd.
Milton Keynes UK
UKOW07f0901130717
305253UK00005B/409/P